ACTION SPORTS

BMX RIDING

Joe Herran and Ron Thomas

CHELSEA HOUSE
PUBLISHERS
A Haights Cross Communications Company
Philadelphia

This edition first published in 2003 in the United States of America by Chelsea House Publishers, a subsidiary of Haights Cross Communications.

Reprinted 2003

Chelsea House Publishers
1974 Sproul Road, Suite 400
Broomall, PA 19008-0914

The Chelsea House world wide web address is www.chelseahouse.com

Library of Congress Cataloging-in-Publication Data
Herran, Joe.
  BMX riding / by Joe Herran and Ron Thomas.
  v. cm. — (Action sports)
  Includes index.
  Contents: What is BMX riding? — BMX gear — Riding safely — Getting ready to ride — Maintaining the bike — Skills, tricks and techniques — The BMX riding scene — In competition — BMX champions — Then and now — Related action sports.
  ISBN 0-7910-7002-6
  1. Bicycle motocross—Juvenile literature. [1. Bicycle motocross. 2. Bicycle racing.] I. Thomas, Ron, 1947- II. Title. III. Action sports (Chelsea House Publishers)
  GV1049.3 .H49 2003
  796.6'2—dc21
                                                                            2002002292

First published in 2002 by
MACMILLAN EDUCATION AUSTRALIA PTY LTD
627 Chapel Street, South Yarra, Australia, 3141

Copyright © Joe Herran and Ron Thomas 2002
Copyright in photographs © individual photographers as credited
Edited by Miriana Dasovic
Text design by Karen Young
Cover design by Karen Young
Illustrations by Nives Porcellato and Andy Craig
Page layout by Raul Diche
Photo research by Legend Images

Printed in China

Acknowledgements
The authors wish to acknowledge and thank Greig Innes for his assistance and advice in the writing of this text.

Cover photo: BMX rider, courtesy of Sport the library.

AAP/AP Photo/Victoria Arocho, p. 29 (right); AAP/AP Photo/Kent C. Horner, p. 26 (right); Australian Picture Library/Corbis, p. 18 (bottom); Australian Picture Library/Empics, pp. 5 (top), 15 (top), 19 (top); Bill Bachman, p. 10; Coo-ee Picture Library, pp. 15 (bottom), 28–29; Getty Images/Allsport, pp. 4, 19 (bottom), 26 (left); Legend Images, pp. 7, 12, 21 (top), 24; Tim Lillethorup/LProductns, p. 28 (left); Blake Peterson/www.momentumfoto.com, p. 27 (left); Dale Mann/Retrospect, pp. 13, 29 (center); Sporting Images, pp. 5 (bottom), 11, 18 (top), 22–23 (all), 30; Sport the library, pp. 5 (center), 8–9, 14, 16, 17, 20, 21 (bottom), 25, 27 (right).

CONTENTS

INTRODUCTION

In this book you will read about:

- BMX bikes
- the gear used by riders
- the features of a BMX track
- the safety measures and rules used to keep riders safe
- tricks and stunts performed by riders
- some of the top BMX riders in competition today
- the history of the sport from its beginnings in the 1970s.

In the beginning

BMX stands for bicycle motocross. BMX racing began in the early 1970s. Some kids in California used their bicycles to imitate cross-country or motocross motorcycle riders. New bikes, which looked like the motocross machines, were soon being made. These new bikes were tough and could be twisted, turned and bumped without falling apart.

BMX riding today

The sport of BMX is enjoyed by the young and not-so-young, male and female alike. BMX has grown in popularity in many countries around the world. Competitions attracting hundreds of professional and **amateur** riders are held every year.

The new-style bikes are high-tech machines. Special shoes and protective clothing have been designed and made for BMX riders as they race or compete in Extreme or X Games. Specially built BMX tracks and **skate parks** in cities and towns around the world are venues for fast-action BMX competitions.

 **Warning** This is not a how-to book for aspiring BMX riders. It is intended as an introduction to the exciting world of BMX riding and a look at where the sport has come from and where it is heading.

WHAT IS BMX RIDING?

There are two types of BMX riding: BMX racing and BMX freestyle.

BMX racing

BMX racing is done on tracks that are typically more than 1,000 feet (300 meters) long. The tracks contain twists, turns and jumps to test a rider's skills.

 BMX races are called **motos** or mains.

BMX freestyle

BMX freestyle can be divided into four major categories: street and mini, **vert**, **flatland** and dirt.

Street and mini

Street competitions involve the rider performing tricks that display smooth, technical and exciting riding. These are done in a street park on a variety of ramps, rails, walls and other obstacles. Mini freestyle takes its name from the mini-ramps used by street riders to do small **airs** and other tricks.

Vert

Vert BMX riders perform the same types of tricks as street riders. Instead of using obstacles on the ground, the vert rider performs tricks in the giant **halfpipe** or vert ramp.

A vert BMX rider does an air in the halfpipe.

Flatland

Flatland involves the rider performing tricks on flat ground, such as spinning in tight circles and **gyrating**. It is acrobatics on a bike.

Dirt

High-speed riding, jumps and big tricks make this type of riding very popular with competitors and spectators alike.

A rider does a big air from a dirt jump.

BMX GEAR

The BMX bike

A BMX bike must be strong enough to withstand the pressures of rough riding but light enough to travel fast and be **maneuverable**. The most common types of BMX bikes are racing, street and flatland.

- Racing bikes are lightweight and designed to be used off-road and ridden at high speeds, and to withstand the jolts of hard landings.
- Street and flatland bikes are made to be even tougher than racing bikes. They have different features from racing bikes, such as front and rear brakes, gyros and axle pegs. The pegs are used by BMX riders doing tricks.

Frame

The frame is the steel tubing that makes up the body of the bicycle. To make the frame, lengths of metal tubing are cut and carefully welded together. The frame is then painted and decorated.

Wheels

In addition to keeping the bike rolling, the wheels on a BMX bike are designed to absorb much of the shock from riding over rough ground and from landing after a jump. The wheels are made up of four parts: tires, spokes, rims and hubs.

BMX tires are wider than most bicycle tires. Street riders and racers use tires with a knobbly surface to give better grip on loose surfaces. Bikes ridden on the ramp use smooth tires. The tires are attached to the rims, which hold the spokes in place. Rims are usually made of an aluminum alloy. The spokes are attached to the rims and the tension, or stiffness, of the spokes determines the strength of the wheel. The hubs are the metal casings that hold the wheel to the fork. The fork holds the front wheel to the frame.

Handlebars

Brake lever

Spokes

Rim

Fork

Peg

Frame

Seat post

Back brake

Sprocket

Chain

Crank

Pedal

RACING BMX BIKE

Pedals, crank and sprockets

Pedals are made of metal and have teeth-like grips on the surface so that the rider's shoes do not slip off. Pedals are attached to the crank, which is attached to the frame. Bearings inside the crank help it turn smoothly. Sprockets have 40 to 48 teeth, which grip the chain.

Brakes

Brakes are fitted to the front and rear wheels, except for racing BMX bikes, which do not have front brakes. The brake handles are located on the grip of the handlebars. A gyro is a cable detangler that is fitted to allow a rider to spin the handlebars without tangling the brake cables.

Seat

Riders in BMX events bounce up and down on the seats as they jump. The seat therefore needs to be both strong and comfortable. Seats are slim with narrow fronts, and are made of nylon. The seat is held to the frame by the seat post and the seat post clamp.

Handlebars

Handlebars come in different sizes and bends. A BMX rider will try many handlebars until finding one that is comfortable and suits the length of the rider's arms. The handlebar stem holds the handlebars to the frame.

Other gear

Helmet

Helmets must be worn in any kind of BMX competition. A full-face helmet that protects the mouth, chin and nose should fit snugly without being tight. (A loose helmet will flop around and drop down over the rider's eyes.) Helmets are usually made of molded plastic, with a foam inner shell and a removable cloth lining. A sun visor is useful and can be clipped to the helmet. Dirt and racing riders often use a face mask on the helmet to stop dirt and dust from flying in their faces.

Gloves

Gloves help a rider grip the handlebars. They are strong and padded to protect the palms, with molded rubber in the fingers for extra protection.

Shirt and pants

Riders wear shirts with long sleeves and any type of jeans or long pants. Many riders prefer to wear racing tops with extra padding and padded track pants for added protection.

Shoes

Specially designed shoes for BMX riding have rubber soles for easy grip on the pedals, and a padded tongue for rider protection and comfort. Air pockets in the heels lessen the impact of rough riding on the rider's feet.

Padding

Knee and shin pads provide extra protection. Pads are usually worn under the pants and have a plastic cup covering the knee. Plastic chest plates are worn by vert and dirt riders to protect the upper body. Many riders also wear pads to protect their elbows and wrists.

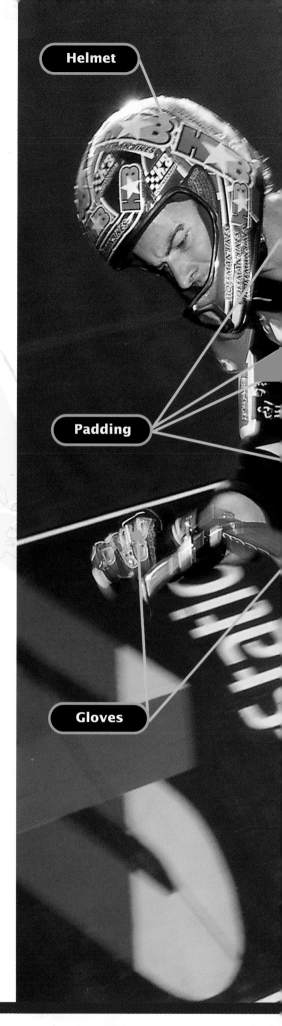

Helmet

Padding

Gloves

Shirt and pants

Shoes

RIDING
SAFELY

Before using their bikes in a BMX competition, riders should always:
- make sure all bolts are tight
- remove all reflectors
- pad their bikes (the top tube, stem and handlebar crossbar)
- wear protective gear (helmet, wrist, elbow and knee guards)
- have the basic skills of speed control, turning, braking and stopping on flat ground
- keep bicycles and protective gear in good working order
- obey the rules made to protect riders and spectators.

When practicing their sport, BMX riders should always:

- practice tricks on a large space with soft ground
- cycle in control at all times
- have someone with them in case of an accident.

To avoid collisions, BMX riders should always keep their heads up and be alert when riding in a skate park. A mistake that is commonly made occurs when a rider drops-in on a mini-ramp at the same time that another rider drops-in from the opposite **deck**.

All skate parks have rules designed to keep riders safe.

The City of Boroondara
JUNCTION
Skate Park

CONDITIONS FOR SAFE USE:
This Path is a Pedestrian Spa

THIS FACILITY IS TO BE USED BY SKATEBOARDERS, ROLLERBLADERS & B BIKE RIDERS IN ACCORDANCE WITH TH FOLLOWING RULES:

- Protective clothing, including helmet, knee & e pads & wrist guards must be worn at all time
- Only skate in designated skate areas - do not on pedestrian paths or footpaths.
- Always skate safely and within your skill le

GETTING READY TO
RIDE

Warming up and keeping fit

Gentle stretching, jogging or jumping will warm up and loosen muscles before taking to the track. Warm, loose muscles work better and are less likely to cramp. Doing some simple exercises before riding may help avoid injuries such as torn ligaments and sprains.

Learning to fall

All riders doing tricks should know how to knee-slide when a trick goes wrong. This is done by falling onto the knee pads and sliding out of danger. A rider should also know how to throw the bike out of the way.

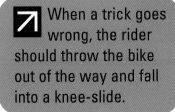 When a trick goes wrong, the rider should throw the bike out of the way and fall into a knee-slide.

MAINTAINING THE BIKE

Tires and wheels

Tires must be kept at the correct air pressure, so they stay hard. Before riding, the tires should be checked for signs of wear or damage. The strength of the wheel depends on the tension of the spokes, so these also need to be checked. The rims that hold the spokes to the wheels need to be cleaned and checked to make sure there are no cracks. When cleaning the rims, the rider should make sure that the brake pads are clean, too.

Crank

The crank transfers the power of the rider's legs to the back wheel and converts it into speed. It should be cleaned often and checked for damage.

↗ A BMX rider tightens a bolt on the axle, which holds the wheel to the frame.

Brakes

Brake levers must be firmly clamped to the handlebars to ensure they work properly. Brake pads must be checked to make sure they are fitted properly.

Chain

The bike's chain must fit properly and be well lubricated. Any type of oil can be used, but too much oil will trap dirt and prevent the chain from working properly.

The BMX rider's toolkit

Having the correct tools makes maintenance easier. Here are some tools often found in a BMX rider's toolkit:

- pliers
- adjustable wrench
- screwdrivers
- spanner
- spoke key
- multi-grip wrench
- allen key set
- hammer
- freewheel remover
- tire levers.

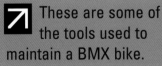
↗ These are some of the tools used to maintain a BMX bike.

↖ The crank should be cleaned regularly. Speed is lost if the crank becomes stiff or dirty.

Screwdrivers

Pliers

Spoke key

Allen key set

Adjustable wrench

SKILLS, TRICKS AND TECHNIQUES

The basics of BMX racing

The race

When the gate snaps down, the race begins. Up to eight riders race down the track in lanes. After the first turn, the riders can leave their lanes and ride anywhere on the track. There are all kinds of jumps and turns to go through before the finishing straight.

The start

At the start of the race, the riders line up with their front wheels resting against a starting gate. This is the starting stance. A race takes only about 30 to 45 seconds, so getting a good start is vital. The instant the gate drops, the riders take off, leaning forward as they pedal hard and fast.

Getting the best start in a race is known as the holeshot.

Turns

When taking a sharp or flat turn, called a sweeper, the rider uses one leg for balance. Banked turns are called berms, and the riders approach them at high speed. These are good places to overtake other riders.

BMX riders must learn to turn fast on rough surfaces. They do this by **pivoting** the hips, hauling on the handlebars, riding upright on the pedals and letting the bike lean farther out than they do.

◤ BMX racers speed around a berm.

Braking

The rider learns to apply the brake carefully to avoid skidding or pitching forward over the handlebars. To stop quickly, the rider puts all their weight on the pedals and back tire.

PEDALING

◢ The balls of the feet should rest on the pedals when pedaling. When coming to jumps or potholes, the rider lifts slightly off the seat and puts most of their weight on the pedals and handlebars. This allows the bike to pivot underneath the rider, reducing the shock on both rider and bike.

Riding the bumps

The BMX racing track has jumps, called bumps. Riders must learn to 'ride the bumps' when racing on these tracks.

Whoops or whoop-de-doos

Whoops are a group of small jumps placed closely together in places along the track. The rider approaches them fast, rapidly rising and falling over them. If there are only a couple of jumps, a rider might try to jump over both of them rather than riding over each one at ground level. With a firm grip on the handlebars, the rider launches the bike into the jump. This may give a speed advantage over competitors who ride the whoops.

Table-tops

Table-tops have a flat top, and steep sides that allow the rider to build up speed during the run-up.

↗ BMX racers ride the whoops in a dirt competition.

↗ The rider speeds up the ramp on a table-top and jumps across the flat top to land on the opposite ramp.

16

BMX racing: the rules

The lanes

BMX racing is held on tracks that are 700 to 1,300 feet (213 to 396 meters) long with twists and turns and obstacles to jump. The riders all start at the top of a hill or ramp, and ride down in lanes. They must stay in their lanes until the first turn.

At the first turn the riders encounter the bumps, whoops and turns. Riders race close together but physical contact is not allowed. Any rider deliberately forcing another rider off the track may be disqualified.

Motos and mains

BMX race organizers have events for riders of all ages, starting as young as six. Riders in each age group are divided into groups of six or eight. They compete in three motos, in different starting positions each time. The most successful riders go through to the next round. In the moto system, one point is awarded for finishing first, two for second and so on. The four riders with the fewest points after their three motos qualify for the next round. The final races are called mains.

Other racing rules

- Helmets must cover the whole face and have a strap attached.
- Enclosed shoes must be worn to protect the feet.
- Long pants (waist to ankles) are compulsory.
- Long-sleeved shirts must be worn, or short-sleeved shirts with sufficient elbow padding.
- Handlebar grips are compulsory.
- All kickstands, chain guards, fenders and reflector brackets must be removed.
- Padding is required on the frame's top tube, stem and handlebar crossbar.
- The bicycle frame and its parts must be in good condition.
- Seats must be securely fastened.
- Riders must not ride in an unsafe manner that endangers others.

After the first turn, the lead rider can take any lane available but is not allowed to block another rider.

Freestyle street tricks

BMX freestyle street events are displays of spins, jumps and maneuvers. Riders must control their bikes and their balance as they perform, making the bikes do what they want. It takes a lot of practice and some courage and determination to perform such tricks.

Wheelie

Balancing or riding on the back wheel is called a wheelie, and it is always done while the rider is pedaling. While standing on the pedals or sitting down, the rider pulls up on the handlebars. This raises the front wheel off the ground while the rider balances on the back wheel. To end the move, the front wheel is allowed to drop to the ground.

Endo

Balancing on the front wheel is called an endo. The rider raises the back wheel into the air, keeping the front wheel rolling. To perform a curb endo, the rider slowly rolls the bike forward toward the curb. When the front tire hits the curb, the rider leans forward until the back wheel leaves the ground.

WHEELIE

ENDO

Bunnyhop

A bunnyhop is a trick in which a jump is done without using anything as a take-off ramp. As the bike moves along a flat surface, the rider crouches on the bike and lifts forward to spring upwards. Both wheels leave the ground, and the rider jumps over an obstacle. It takes practice, but some riders can jump long distances doing the bunnyhop.

Barspin

While the bike is moving, the rider stands on the pedals and pulls into a **manual**. This lifts the front wheel off the ground. Crossing hands on the handlebars, the rider spins the handlebars and catches them again before the front wheel lands.

BUNNYHOP

BARSPIN

Flatland freestyle tricks

Flatland tricks consist of spins, jumps and balances performed on an area of flat land. Flatland riding requires good timing and rhythm, great balance and lots of patience. It takes time to learn flatland maneuvers.

To perform flatland tricks, the rider begins by balancing on the pedals, handlebars or pegs. The rider then lifts the bike wheels off the ground, kicks the bike away and catches it again, spins the handlebars, and does wheelies, endos and other tricks. These tricks have names such as 'the backyard', 'grasshopper and crickets', 'rockwalk' and 'gut walker'. The bike keeps moving backwards and forwards throughout the tricks. A flatland competitor must link all the tricks together in a fluid display of skill.

↗ Flatland tricks are like acrobatics on a bike.

↖ Lots of practice is needed to perfect a trick.

Freestyle tricks on a ramp

Freestyle also includes tricks in the halfpipe or on mini-ramps. Riders shoot skywards above the ramp to twist, swivel and flip in midair. They also **grind** along the **coping** of the halfpipe.

Beginning on the ramp

Beginning riders start on smaller ramps where they learn how to ride **transitions**. They try basic **carves** without lifting the wheels to get a feel for **pumping** transitions, moving both forwards and backwards.

Roll-in

A roll-in is how a rider gets from the deck to the transition of the ramp. The rider rolls down one side of the ramp to the other side. Alternatively, the rider can do a peg stall. The peg on the bike is placed on the coping and the rider then rolls-in to the transition.

ROLL-IN

Experienced riders roll-in straight from the deck. While standing on the pedals, they bend their knees and turn their wheels straight into the ramp's transition.

No footer

This trick is performed in the air above the ramp. When airborne, the rider takes both feet off the pedals and stretches them sideways before bringing them back to the pedals for landing.

NO FOOTER

Dirt jumping tricks

All of these tricks are performed in the air.

One footer

Once in the air, the rider takes one foot off the pedal and kicks it out to the side before bringing it back to the pedal for landing.

One hander

In this trick, the rider takes one hand off the handlebars when in the air. Two hands off the handlebars is called a no hander. Another variation is the one hander, no footer.

KICKOUT

When the back wheel leaves the top of a jump, the rider swings the rear of the bike out to the right or left by using the hips and legs. The rear of the bike swings out to the side before the rider pulls it back in for the landing.

 Once in the air, the rider takes one foot off the pedal and swings it across the top tube of the bike. Both legs are then on the same side of the tube. Before landing, the rider swings the leg back over the top tube and onto the pedal.

THE NOTHING

 The rider takes both hands and feet off the bike while in the air so that no part of the body touches the bike! The rider then catches the bike in midair and lands.

THE BMX RIDING
SCENE

BMX bike riding is popular throughout the world. Many communities in the United States, Australia and Europe have local BMX clubs. These clubs organize races and other competitions and teach riders how to care for their bikes. Competitions are organized in age groups for both boys and girls, starting at about six years of age. Older riders compete as well, and they help teach younger riders about racing and how to do freestyle tricks.

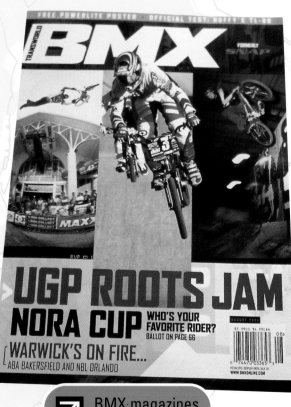

BMX magazines contain new tricks and information about the BMX world.

Finding out more about BMX riding

You can find out more about the sport from magazines such as *BMX Plus!* and *Ride BMX*. They feature information about riders and competitions and discuss the latest developments in the design of BMX bikes. Almost all bike manufacturers and companies making safety equipment and clothing advertise in them. Riders can order bike parts and other equipment from these companies. Some of the magazines have websites where interested people can log-on to find the latest BMX news and more information about all aspects of BMX racing. Equipment can be ordered over the internet. Videos that show riders how to do tricks are also available.

IN COMPETITION

Freestyle competitions

While some BMX riders specialize in racing, others compete in several freestyle events. There are street and dirt competitions, and vert competitions on the ramp.

Freestyle competitors go through prepared routines that include tricks, movements and balances. Tricks done in the air are called aerials.

Judging

Judges award points for:

- control of the bike
- a rider's skill in performing the tricks
- the number of tricks performed
- the difficulty of the tricks
- the way all the tricks are linked together.

Time limits

Each routine has a time limit set by the organizers. The rider performs as many tricks as possible in that time. Vert displays usually last only 50 or 60 seconds. Flatland competitors may perform for up to 5 minutes. Dirt competitors race against the clock, performing jumps and aerials along the way. Times and the competition requirements may vary, depending on what the event organizers want.

Freestyle competitions are displays of a rider's skills.

Types of competitions

There are many professional freestyle competitions held each year around the world including the World Championships, the X Games and the Gravity Games. Local BMX bike clubs hold competitions for bike riders of all ages.

BMX
CHAMPIONS

Top BMX riding champions come from all over the world including Japan, Australia, Europe and South America. However, most of the top riders come from the United States.

↗ Dave Mirra

- Nicknamed 'Miracle Boy'
- Rides freestyle BMX (vert and street)
- Born April 4, 1974
- Lives in Greenville, North Carolina
- Began competing in 1987

Career highlights

- Dave has won more medals than any other BMX rider. He has competed in both vert and street competitions in the X Games since 1995, and he has come first or second in every competition. At the 1999 Gravity Games, he won both the vert and street competitions.
- Dave has a computer game named after him, and he has his own skate park.
- He performed the first ever double back flip in competition in 2000.
- His nickname comes about because he has survived being hit by a car (1993) and a serious crash during competition (1995), after which his doctors said he would never ride again. He does still!

↗ Mat Hoffman

- Nicknamed 'The Condor'
- Rides vert
- Born September 1, 1972
- Lives in Oklahoma City, Oklahoma
- Began competing in 1984

Career highlights

- X Games: 2000 vert – bronze; 1999 vert – seventh; 1997 vert – bronze; 1996 vert – gold; 1995 vert – gold; Mat was the World Champion from 1987 until 1994.
- He has placed first or second at all events he entered in 2000.
- Mat owns his own bike company and there is a computer game named after him, *Mat Hoffman's Pro BMX*.

↗ Colin Mackay

- Rides street and dirt
- Born August 18, 1978
- Lives in Brisbane, Australia
- Began competing in 1993

Career highlights

- In 1999, he was one of two Australians to compete in Bike Stunt at the X Games.
- In 1999, he took first place in the street competition and second place in the dirt competition at the Australian X Games.
- In 1998, he took third place in the street competition and second place in the dirt competition at the Australian X Games.
- In 2000, he took eighth place in the street competitions at the X trials in Nashville and fifth place at street competitions in Florida.

↗ Ryan Nyquist

- Rides dirt, street and vert
- Born March 6, 1979
- Lives in Los Gatos, California
- Began competing in 1995

Career highlights

- 1997 X Games: dirt – bronze; street – fifth
- 1998 X Games: dirt – silver; street – fourth; vert – 15th; vert doubles – fourth
- 1999 X Games: dirt – bronze; street – fifth; vert – ninth. This result made him the only rider ever to get a place in the top 10 in dirt, vert and street competitions at the X Games.
- 2000 X Games: dirt – gold
- In 2000 he also won dirt competitions in Pittsburgh.
- In 2002, won his first X Games park riding gold medal.

THEN AND NOW

Early 1970s	Mid-1970s	1974	1975
BMX racing began when some teenagers in California used their bicycles to imitate cross-country or motocross motorcycle riders. Among them were Scot Breithaupt and Ernie Alexander, considered the founders of BMX.	New bicycles that looked like the motocross motorcycles were made. These new bikes were tough and could be twisted, turned and bumped without falling apart. Scot Breithaupt and Ernie Alexander built a home-made track, similar to the motorcycle motocross tracks. They then organized other teenagers to race their bikes on it.	The National Bicycle League was formed in the United States. It turned backyard racing into a competitive sport with formal rules, performed on local, state, national and international levels.	The first organized BMX bike racing events were held in the United States

Mid-1970s

1979	1980s	1990s	1995	1999

cle companies
ized there was a
wing market for
X bikes so more
es were
nufactured.

Improved BMX tracks were built. These were longer and wider with a greater number of jumps.

BMX makers built stronger bikes using chromoly.

Local BMX racing organizations were set up to run events and race meetings.

Professional BMX racing began, and freestyle trick riding began on flatland and in the halfpipe.

BMX bike clubs grew throughout the world.

Freestyle BMX riding became an event in the X Games.

BMX Freestyle became part of the Gravity Games.

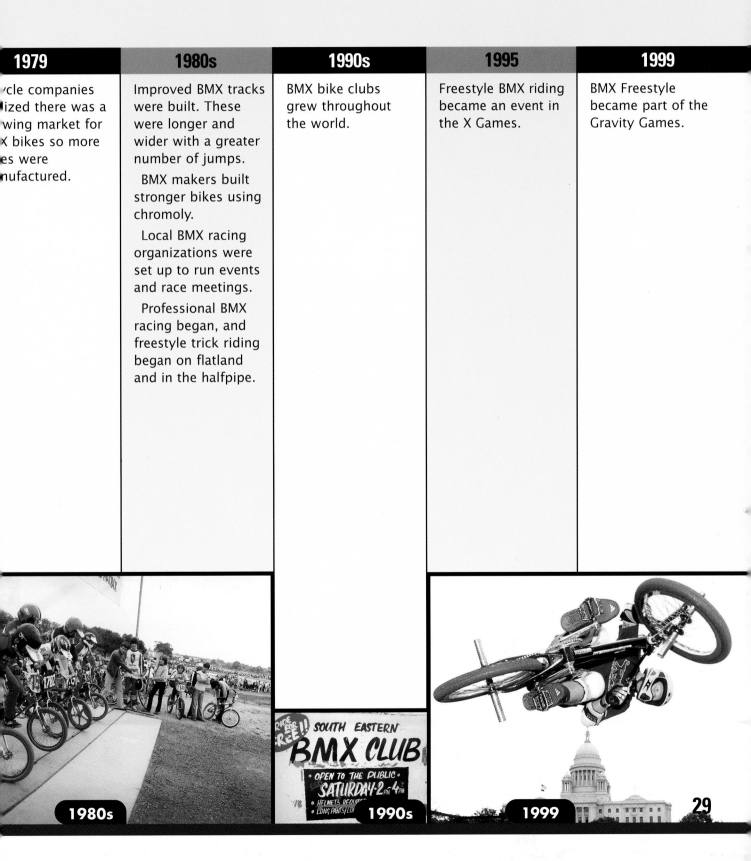

1980s

RIDE FOR FREE!! SOUTH EASTERN
BMX CLUB
• OPEN TO THE PUBLIC •
SATURDAY • 2PM – 4PM
• HELMETS REQUIRED •
• LONG PANTS / LO

1990s

1999

29

RELATED ACTION
SPORTS

Mountain bike riding and mountain scootering are sports that contain elements of BMX riding.

Mountain bike riding

Mountain biking was developed in the mid-1970s in hilly country just outside San Francisco. The first mountain bike race took place on October 21, 1976. In 1977, a bike racer and bike builder named Joe Breeze became the first person to build a mountain bike using the stiffer and lighter chromoly materials, which had been used to build road racing bikes. By 1983, the first mass-produced mountain bikes were being sold.

Some mountain bike events

- Cross-country – competitors race against each other and the clock for the best time over rough ground. Cross-country racing became an Olympic event in the Atlanta Olympics in 1996.
- Downhill racing – riders race down a slope at speeds that can exceed 60 miles (97 kilometers) per hour. Crashes happen very often!
- In dual **slalom** racing, one rider races against another down a course, making a number of tight turns on the way to the finish.

↗ Mountain bike riders race over rough ground.

Mountain scootering

Mountain scootering combines BMX, mountain biking, skiing and skateboarding. The scooter has the handlebars, wheels and brakes of a bike, the deck of a skateboard, and the bottom (flat surface) of a ski. The mountain scooter is used for downhill races as well as for skateboard-style grinds and tricks.

GLOSSARY

airs tricks performed while the rider is airborne

amateur an athlete who has never competed for money

carve a turn

coping the metal tube at the top edge of the halfpipe

deck the top of the ramp

flatland freestyle tricks performed on the ground

grind a move in which the rider jumps onto something and slides along it on the bike

gyrating moving from side to side

halfpipe a U-shaped ramp

maneuverable able to move skilfully

manual a stand-up wheelie done without pedaling

moto a qualifying round at a BMX race. The riders who do the best in their motos can then transfer to the mains

pivoting turning from side to side

pumping to gain speed on the ramp

skate park a park with ramps and obstacles on which BMX riders can do tricks

slalom a downhill race zigzagging between obstacles

transition the part of the ramp that is curved

vert a ramp

INDEX